The Campus History Series

Gannon University

On the Front Cover: The graduating class of 1953 entered Gannon in a time of peace, but less than a year later, the United States was again at war. Many of the students were World War II veterans attending college on the GI bill and left before finishing their degree to serve their country once again. (Courtesy of Gannon University.)

Cover Background: Villa Maria College's Millcreek Township campus was located on 45 acres of land and included shaded walkways, open lawns, and athletic fields. It consisted of 10 buildings, including two residence halls, a library with 50,000 volumes, a gymnasium and natatorium, and an adult learning center. (Courtesy of Gannon University.)

The Campus History Series

Gannon University

Greg Czarnecki

ISBN 978-1-4671-0377-0

Published by Arcadia Publishing
Charleston, South Carolina

Printed in the United States of America

Library of Congress Control Number: 2019935110

For all general information, please contact Arcadia Publishing:
Telephone 843-853-2070
Fax 843-853-0044
E-mail sales@arcadiapublishing.com
For customer service and orders:
Toll-Free 1-888-313-2665

Visit us on the Internet at www.arcadiapublishing.com

This book is dedicated to my wife, Karen, and daughter Tara, who are also a part of the Gannon family.

Contents

ACKNOWLEDGMENTS

Many people made this book possible. Most of the photographs and the stories behind them came from the pages of the Gannon and Villa Maria yearbooks and Gannon's newspaper the *Gannon Knight*. Without their writers and photographers, much of the Gannon and Villa Maria stories would be lost to history.

This book also would not have been possible without those who worked to save, categorize, and make this history available. Special thanks go to Bob Dobiesz, retired Gannon archivist, who spent years preserving these photographs, and Lori Grossholz, Gannon's current archivist. Lori and her dedicated interns, who spent many hours culling the archives for the photographs you see here, made researching this book a joy.

Thanks also go to the staff of the Alumni Association and the university advancement office, especially Nancy Bird and Allison Mosier. When I first pitched the idea to Nancy, she jumped at the chance to help make it happen and build support within the university. I cannot thank Allison enough for all the work that she and her interns did in producing the high-quality scans of the photographs in this book.

Also included in this volume are photographs of Gannon's more recent growth and expansion. Thanks to Andy Lapiska of Gannon's marketing and communication department for these beautiful photographs. Dave Rung of the athletics department provided many of the photographs in the athletics chapter, and Mark Gaeta's encyclopedic knowledge of Gannon's sports made that chapter possible.

Finally, I would like to thank Gannon's president, Dr. Keith Taylor, and his outstanding executive staff not only for supporting this project, but more importantly, for continuing Gannon's rich history and for plotting a future that promises to be even more remarkable than its past.

All photographs in this book were provided courtesy of Gannon University.

Introduction

John Mark Gannon was installed as bishop of the Roman Catholic Diocese of Erie in 1920. It was a time of rapid growth in the diocese as Catholic immigrants coming from Poland, Italy, and the Slavic countries necessitated the opening of many new parishes and parish schools. As the number of students graduating from the schools grew, so did demand for Catholic high schools and colleges.

The Sisters of St. Joseph opened Villa Maria Academy High School in 1892, and in keeping with the Catholic school norm at the time, it was for girls only. To accommodate the boys, Bishop Gannon established Cathedral Preparatory School in 1921. The school was located in the basement of St. Peter's Cathedral and graduated its first class in 1925. Many of the graduates came from poor families and could not afford to go away to college. Bishop Gannon believed that the right to a college education should not be based on wealth or social standing and that the boys of Erie should "receive an education at a minimal cost—a cost they can well defray with a paper route."

Msgr. "Doc" Wehrle was the person who Bishop Gannon entrusted to advance his vision of Catholic education for the diocese. He was the headmaster of Cathedral Prep, the superintendent of schools in the Erie diocese, and the president of Villa Maria College, a women's college founded by the Sisters of St. Joseph in 1925.

Since there was no local college for the boys graduating from Cathedral Prep, Monsignor Wehrle asked the sisters to accept them as students at Villa Maria College, and they reluctantly agreed. The arrangement lasted for two years until the sisters asked that they not return. It was clear that a Catholic college for men was needed.

Doc Wehrle's solution was to open a branch campus of Villa Maria College for men in downtown Erie. Cathedral College, as it was named, opened in 1933 during the depth of the Great Depression and was housed in a dilapidated building next to Cathedral Prep, which shared some of the space. The college never granted a degree. It was a community college whose sole purpose was to provide students with two years of low-cost schooling in preparation for transfer to a four-year college.

The relationship with Villa Maria College ended just a year later when the women's college learned that in order to be accredited it must sever its ties with Cathedral College. Monsignor Wehrle then approached Duquesne University in Pittsburgh to see if it would sponsor the fledgling community college, but it declined. He found a savior in his alma mater, Saint Vincent College in Latrobe, Pennsylvania.

Cathedral College operated under the Saint Vincent charter until 1941, when it moved to a new home, got a new name, and once again was operating under the charter of Villa Maria College. Bishop Gannon surprised everyone in the city of Erie when he announced that the Gannon School of Arts and Science would be moving into what had been one of Erie's most elegant homes, the Scott-Strong Mansion. The mansion had been empty for five years and was destined to become a parking lot before Gannon gave it new life.

William Lawrence Scott, a successful businessman, two-term mayor of Erie, and US congressman, began construction of the 46-room mansion in 1881. He passed away before what is today Gannon's Old Main was completed, but his daughter Annie and her husband, Charles Hamot Strong, lived in the home for many years. The mansion came with several adjacent buildings including stables and servants' quarters that are still a part of the university today.

When it opened in September 1941, the Gannon School of Arts and Science had 400 students, four times more than Cathedral College had ever enrolled. A little more than two months later, enrollment plummeted to just 50 students when Japan bombed Pearl Harbor, and many of the students left to fight in World War II. The school struggled, but due to the hard work of Monsignor Wehrle and the small but dedicated faculty and staff, it not only survived, it was able to obtain its own charter. In 1944, it began awarding four-year degrees. Gannon College was born.

Once the war ended, enrollment swelled as returning soldiers took advantage of the GI bill, which provided them with a free education. It was clear that the school needed more room. Over the next two decades, Gannon underwent rapid growth both physically and in the number of degrees and academic programs it offered. It went from a small college housed in one building to a major property owner and employer in the city of Erie.

Villa Maria College was also growing. After it outgrew its original campus on Erie's west side, the Sisters of St. Joseph moved the college to a beautiful campus in nearby Millcreek Township. Enrollment, which also plummeted during World War II, rebounded, and the number of academic degrees and programs grew significantly through the 1960s.

The 1960s were a time of cultural change in the country, and Gannon was not immune. While Erie had three Catholic colleges, none were coeducational, and that was what most students wanted. In 1964, Gannon began admitting women on a limited basis, primarily in programs not offered by Villa Maria or Mercyhurst Colleges. Not wanting to compete with the other two schools, they were only accepted into the afternoon and evening divisions and were referred to as "non-male evening students taking day classes." In 1969, that distinction disappeared when Gannon began admitting women into all of its programs and majors.

The biggest change for Gannon in the 1970s occurred in 1979. On December 19, Pennsylvania governor Richard Thornburgh came to Erie to announce that Gannon College had been granted university status, and Gannon University was born.

In 1989, a task force composed of trustees from Gannon University and Villa Maria College formed to study whether a "total and combined effort" between Gannon and Villa was "feasible and advantageous to assure the future of quality Catholic higher education in the Diocese of Erie." The team concluded that it was, and on July 1, 1989, the two schools merged. Villa Maria became a college within Gannon University, and Villa's president, Sister Leonic Shanley, became the dean of the college and one of Gannon's vice presidents. Villa continued to operate for a time on its Millcreek campus but eventually relocated to Gannon's downtown campus. Gannon's nursing program is today called the Villa Maria School of Nursing.

For more than 90 years, Gannon has grown in size, academic offerings, and its impact on the Erie community. In 2015, that influence expanded when the Ruskin, Florida, campus opened. The campus, which offers graduate degrees in health sciences, is already undergoing a major expansion.

Archbishop Gannon had a vision for a college for the poor boys of Erie. Now a century later, no one could have envisioned what an impact the school would have on generations of men and women of the city of Erie and beyond. This book offers a snapshot, however incomplete, of how that vision unfolded.

One

The Early Years

Cathedral College occupied a portion of this building, the former home of wealthy Erieite Jerome Francis Downing, at 225 West Ninth Street from 1933 to 1941. In addition to classrooms, the building also housed administrative offices and a library for Cathedral Prep, and was Monsignor Wehrle's residence. The building was torn down in 1944.

Graduates of Cathedral College never earned a degree. It was a school where students could take two years of college courses in three programs—science, liberal arts, and business—inexpensively and then transfer to a four-year college to finish their degree. The courses they took were often based on the curriculum of the target colleges where many of them would

ultimately go. One of those colleges was Saint Vincent College in Latrobe, Pennsylvania. Saint Vincent was Monsignor Wehrle's alma mater, and because of his close ties with the school, Cathedral College operated under its charter from 1934 to 1941. Cathedral College never exceeded more than 100 students or nine faculty members at a time.

Bishop John Mark Gannon was born in Erie in 1877, the seventh of nine children. Before studying for the priesthood, he graduated from Clark's Business College and worked as a bookkeeper at Erie City Ironworks. He was ordained in 1901 and served in several parishes in the Erie diocese, the last being St. Andrew's in Erie while he was an auxiliary bishop. He was installed as bishop of the Diocese of Erie in 1920, making him one of the youngest bishops in the country. Education was a cornerstone of his tenure, and he worked hard to fulfill the mandate of the Council of Baltimore, which was to establish a school in every parish. In addition to the many grade schools he started, he founded Cathedral Preparatory High School as well as Cathedral College and its successors, the Gannon School of Arts and Science and Gannon College.

In 1925, Bishop Gannon and the Sisters of St. Joseph broke ground for Gannon Hall, the first dedicated home for Villa Maria College (above). The building was located adjacent to Villa Maria High School, which opened in 1892, and the sister's motherhouse, at the corner of Eighteenth and Liberty Streets in Erie. Our Lady's Chapel on the southern end of the building (below) was dedicated on July 27, 1927.

In 1927, two years after Villa Maria College opened, it dedicated its new building, Gannon Hall. The significance of the event was demonstrated by the attendance of Rev. Pietro Fumasoni-Biondi, the apostolic delegate to the United States. In this role, he was an official envoy of the Holy See, a position analogous to a foreign ambassador. Five years later, he was appointed a cardinal by Pope Pius XI.

Bishop's Day, pictured here in 1942, was described in the Villa Maria yearbook *Mariole*: "His Excellency Bishop John Mark Gannon serves not only as Chancellor of Villa Maria College but as its steadfast friend and shepherd. Upon the occasion of his annual visit to the college Bishop Gannon joins, in true Christ-like spirit, the rejoicing of his flock and begs that they, as Catholic Women, lead good Christian lives."

In 1881, William Lawrence Scott began construction of a 46-room mansion on Perry Square in downtown Erie. Scott was a successful businessman who had amassed a fortune from coal, steel, railroading, shipping, and land development. While he passed away before the mansion was completed, his daughter Annie and her husband lived there for many years. The mansion, which today is Gannon's Old Main, was arguably the most opulent of the many such homes that were built along Sixth Street in what today is referred to as millionaire's row. The mansion also had several associated buildings for servants and a state-of-the-art carriage house that included a pulley-operated elevator that could lift and store the family's many carriages on multiple floors. When Annie died in 1934, she left the mansion to her sister, who abandoned the home two years later when she moved to New York. When Bishop Gannon purchased the building in 1941, the city was considering razing it and making the property a parking lot.

Annie Wainwright Scott (left), the daughter of William Lawrence Scott, married Charles Hamot Strong (below) in 1881. The marriage brought together two of the wealthiest 19th-century Erie families. Strong's family had been instrumental in founding Erie's first hospital, Hamot Hospital, and he was president of the Erie & Pittsburgh Railroad as well as several electric companies and two of Erie's newspapers. The marriage was an unhappy one, and the couple were estranged much of the time, eventually splitting in 1920. Even after their separation, she continued to financially support Hamot hospital and founded the city's first nursing school, the Hamot Hospital Training School for Nurses.

The Strong mansion was the center of Erie's social scene in the late 1800s and early 1900s. In this photograph, Annie and Charles Strong, at center, are celebrating with their families in the mansion's dining room, which today is the university president's office.

Gannon's original chapel was located in the west end of the first floor in what was the Strong Mansion dining room. It was moved to the location seen here when the new library annex was constructed and connected to the west end of the building. This room, which is one of the most striking in Old Main, is covered in gold leaf. Today, it is used as a reception room for events in the adjacent board room.

In 1945, one year after the formation of Gannon College, Bishop Gannon founded St. Mark's Seminary on East Third Street in the former St. Joseph's orphan asylum, which was built in 1871. It provided an atmosphere of piety and discipline for the young men from Cathedral Prep High School and Gannon College who were studying for the priesthood. When it opened, it was home to 19 high school students and one Gannon student, but by 1957, it had swelled to 93 college seminarians, who were affectionately referred to as Markians. In 1960, Bishop Gannon realized one of his dreams when the new St. Mark's Seminary opened on 22 acres of land in southeast Erie.

On the evening of February 10, 1943, a departure ceremony was held in Old Main for 27 students leaving the Gannon School of Arts and Sciences for US Army Reserve training in New Cumberland, Pennsylvania. The ceremony was held in the chapel, which today is the president's office, while more than 500 parents, family, and friends looked on from the corridor. Bishop Gannon predicted that "within a year's time every one of the 27 students should be back in Gannon pursuing their chosen careers where they had been impinged upon by the war." The bishop presented each of the men with a prayer book and rosary. After the ceremony, a banquet was held in Old Main's ballroom followed by a dance in the school auditorium.

The Strong Mansion ballroom is one of the building's most ornate spaces, featuring a ceiling with hand-painted cherubs peering from behind clouds. It has been repurposed many times since Gannon purchased the building in 1941. It served as the school's first library (above) until the new library and commons building was built in 1948. In the 1950s, it served as the registrar's office (below). Today, it serves as the board of trustees' boardroom and also hosts some of the university's formal events such as the Villa Maria College Alumnae High Tea and the Heritage Society Luncheon.

Gannon's first Student Union opened in March 1957 in what was formerly the Julius G. Siegel Mansion on West Sixth Street. This was the first Gannon building dedicated solely to student activities and had two clergy members in residence, serving as supervisors. The furnishings for the building were purchased with the proceeds from Gannon's first winter carnival. Today, the mansion is home to the Erie Community Foundation.

Seen here in 1960, the Gannon Glee Club was formed in 1957. The group performed at various events on campus, made joint appearances with glee clubs from Mercyhurst College and St. John's College of Cleveland, and even appeared on television several times. Rev. Richard Sullivan, who taught in the theology department, was the group's director.

In 1958, Gannon's young men could fill their free time by joining one of the college's two Greek fraternities, Delta Sigma Phi or Tau Kappa Epsilon, or by joining one of 13 clubs, ranging from the Young Democrats League and Young Republicans to the Science Club and Chess Club.

The Spanish Club, seen here in 1958, was founded in 1948 by Eron de Leon Soto to promote the cultural study of the Spanish language and increase interest in Spanish-American relations. Every year, the club observed Pan-American Week by hosting a banquet and participating in activities with the Local International Institute.

The National Society of Pershing Rifles was founded by Gen. John "Black Jack" Pershing, commander of US forces during World War I. It is a military-oriented honor society that aims to develop skills in leadership, military science, and discipline. Gannon's chapter was founded in 1957; in 1959, when this photograph was taken, it hosted the battalion drill competition, competing with chapters from the University of Pittsburgh, Duquesne University, and Washington and Jefferson College.

Archbishop Gannon and Msgr. Wilfred Nash, Gannon's second president, review the college's 10-year plan in this photograph from November 1959. The next decade saw dramatic growth and change for the school, including the addition of graduate programs, accreditation of the engineering programs, admission of the first female students, and the building of Dale Hall, Beyer Hall, the Gannon Theater, and the Zurn Science Center.

In 1959, Monsignor Nash initiated a $4 million development program with the goal of building a multipurpose building, a faculty residence, a new dorm for out-of-town students, and a field house for the school's athletic programs. To help fund this expansion, Nash undertook the school's first large-scale appeal to the Erie community. Many prominent Erie citizens contributed, including Henry Fish, CEO and president of American Sterilizer, one of Erie's largest employers at the time.

On November 29, 1960, ground was broken for a new multipurpose building on the site of the former Fisher Hotel, which was being used for student housing and a cafeteria. Beyer Hall was completed in 1962 at a cost of about $1 million. It contained classrooms, offices, laboratories, a greenhouse, conference rooms, and cafeteria. The snack bar in the basement was especially popular with commuter students, who referred to it as "the scrounge."

By 1956, Gannon College encompassed 15 buildings, including a library and commons, an engineering building, and an auditorium. As the "Junior Prom Headquarters" shows, however, Old Main was still a focal point for the college's 1,000 students.

Since the earliest days of both colleges, there was a special tie between the women of Villa Maria and the men of Gannon, especially at social events. These students are promoting Villa's 1960 Spring Fling to the Gannon student body. The May event included a dance at the Kahkwa Club, dinner at the Beachcomber Inn, a sock hop, and a picnic on Presque Isle.

The biggest social event in Erie's collegiate community in 1960 was the Winter Carnival. Although it was held at Gannon, Villa Maria, and Mercyhurst Colleges, the Saint Vincent College of Nursing also took part. While much of the three-day event occurred in the auditorium, where games and booths were set up, the Italian restaurant put on by the Tau Kappa Epsilon fraternity was also a very popular part of the carnival.

Each spring during Lent, the *Lance*, Gannon's yearbook, sponsored the St. Patrick's Day Dance. As seen in this photograph from 1960, the dance drew large crowds, and all of the money raised went to publishing the yearbook. The highlight of the dance was the crowning of Miss Lance. The candidates were nominated by the yearbook staffs from Gannon, Mercyhurst College, Villa Maria College, and Saint Vincent's Nursing School.

A group of sophomores crowd the cafeteria lunch counter in 1950. The cafeteria was in the basement of the Old Main Annex, which was the first new building constructed on the Gannon campus in 1948. Today, this is the basement of the Keim Commons.

Unlike today's board of trustees, which includes both lay people and clergy, the board was originally comprised exclusively of clergy members selected from across the Diocese of Erie, as seen here in 1964. From left to right are Monsignor Gooder, Bishop McManaman, Father Pesoni, Monsignor Nash, Archbishop Gannon, Monsignor Stanczak, and Father Cebelinski.

The library was the first new building constructed on the campus of Gannon College. When completed in 1948, it already had more than 30,000 volumes. It was made possible by a fundraising campaign that collected $212,000 from the people of Erie. While no longer a library today, it is still heavily used by students and staff for special events and is now the Monsignor Addison B. Yehl Alumni Room. Pictured below is Rita Ann Nies, a Villa Maria alumnus who began working in the Gannon library in 1946, when it was still located in Old Main. She retired in 1985 as the reference librarian for the Nash Library.

The Gannon Institute of Social Action was located at 209 West Sixth Street, in what had formerly been a faculty residence. The institute was established by the Mission Helpers of the Sacred Heart to provide social services and adult education programs to the African American and immigrant communities. The building was demolished in 1956 to make room for the construction of Wehrle Hall.

Beginning in 1959, the Tau Kappa Epsilon fraternity sponsored an annual concert at the Gannon Auditorium. The featured performers for 1963 were Jim Pike, Tony Butala, and Bob Engemann, better known as the Lettermen. Tickets to see the trio perform their hits, including "When I Fall in Love" and "The Way You Look Tonight," ranged from $1.25 for general admission to $2.75 for reserved seats. The group appeared in the auditorium again in 1975.

The St. Thomas More Club was founded in 1960 to train Gannon students interested in becoming members of the lay apostolate. The group below is leaving for a six-week trip to Puerto Rico to perform missionary work, assist with parish censuses, and visit the leper colony at St. Martin. In addition to training for missionary work overseas, the club sponsored events such as the Mad Hatter's Ball, intramural sports teams, and programs for orphans at St. Joseph's home. They also took their message to the Erie community through their own variety show on WICU-TV called *TV for God*.

The freshman class of 1959 would see many changes at Gannon before they graduated. On the national stage, John F. Kennedy was elected president and Ford introduced the Mustang. Closer to home, Beyer Hall, Dale Hall, and the Gannon Theater all became part of the Gannon campus. The athletics program added cross-country as a new intercollegiate sport, and the bowling team won the 1962 national championship. The campus newspaper, the *Gannon Knight,* was awarded "All-American" status by the Catholic Press Association. The Pennsylvania Board of Education also authorized Gannon to award graduate degrees in English, social studies, education, and guidance and counseling.

The current student-run newspaper, the *Gannon Knight*, has been in publication since 1948. Its predecessors were the *Tower*, the Cathedral College paper; the *Mansion*, 1945; and the *Gannonite*, 1946–1948. The university has digitized all of these publications, and they are available online. The paper is published 24 times a year and has a circulation of 2,000. Here, from left to right, staff writers Ray Case and Paul Karg meet with printer Clint Rogers in 1956. Among the headlines that year were the building of a new dorm, Wehrle Hall, and a new food service system, which included steam tables and faster service that allowed students to make their own toast and pour their own coffee.

Two

People

Jim Freeman was a legendary math teacher who began teaching at Cathedral Prep in 1934, taught at Cathedral College, and then at Gannon College beginning in 1945. He was beloved by his students for his friendly, easy-going manner and his ability to make algebra, trigonometry, and calculus understandable for even the most mathematically challenged students. At the time of his death in 1980, he was still teaching at both Gannon and Cathedral Prep. Freeman Hall apartments were named in his honor.

Msgr. Joseph "Doc" Wehrle was a foundational figure in Catholic education in Erie, simultaneously serving as the superintendent of schools for the Diocese of Erie, headmaster of Cathedral Preparatory School, and president of Villa Maria College. He was born in Punxsutawney, Pennsylvania, on September 15, 1891, and ordained in 1915. Doc was known as a generous man who did not hesitate to spend his own earnings, especially during the Depression, to cover institutional expenses, and was notoriously absent-minded. In 1933, he established Cathedral College, which evolved into the Gannon School of Arts and Sciences in 1941, and then Gannon College in 1944. Doc Wehrle served as the college's president from 1933 until his retirement in 1956. He passed away on Christmas Day 1967.

Msgr. Wilfred J. Nash, pictured here in 1957, was a member of the first graduating class of Cathedral College. He was born in Erie on September 8, 1915, attended St. Mary's grade school and graduated from Cathedral Preparatory School in 1933. Not having the funds to attend a four-year college, he enrolled in the inaugural class of Cathedral College, leaving after two years to attend Catholic University. Upon his ordination in 1942, he returned to his alma mater, now called Gannon College, eventually becoming dean of the college in 1950 and serving as president from 1956 to 1977. He oversaw a massive expansion of the school's academic programs and facilities and paved the way for its transition to a university. The university's library bears his name.

Mother Aurelia A'Hearn was born in Lyons, Colorado, and entered the Sisters of St. Joseph in 1923. She spent the next 18 years teaching, including as the head of the Latin department at Villa Maria Academy. In 1942, she was appointed the new general superior of the Sisters of St. Joseph and the second president of Villa Maria College, succeeding Monsignor Wehrle upon his appointment as president of the new Gannon College. During her tenure as Villa's president, the college significantly expanded the number of majors and the size of the student body, and moved to a new 45-acre campus in Millcreek Township. She is pictured here receiving a $500,000 check from Archbishop Gannon in 1960 on the centennial of the founding of the Sisters of St. Joseph.

Dr. Richard Beyer, born in 1905, was the son of a well-known Erie jeweler. After earning a PhD in colonial American history from the University of Iowa, he chaired the history department at Southern Illinois University before coming to Gannon in 1945. At the time of his unexpected death in 1966, he was the history department chair and had also served as the director of the graduate faculty of the social sciences. He was a prolific author and moderated the *Gannon Roundtable Series* on TV and radio. In his honor, the history department hosts the Richard Beyer Memorial Lecture every year. He received the Distinguished Faculty Award posthumously in 1984, and Beyer Hall bears his name.

Rev. Casimir J. Lubiak was born in Wilkes-Barre, Pennsylvania, on October 7, 1915, and attended Cathedral College from 1935 to 1937. He joined the Gannon College faculty in 1949 and became the library director in 1956, succeeding Father Lorei, who had been appointed dean of humanities. Lubiak is best known as the designer of the Nash Learning Resource Center. Among the new features he included were lower-level gardens, a media center, and the university archives, which contain several special collections that he was instrumental in acquiring. In recognition of his years of service, Lubiak was the subject of Gannon's first annual celebrity roast in 1983. He retired in 1980 and passed away in 1985. The Lubiak Apartments on Peach Street were named in his honor.

Owen Thomas Finegan joined Gannon's education department in 1948 as its first director. During his tenure at Gannon, he served as director of guidance and placement, director of student personnel services, and as the dean of pure and applied sciences. He was also one of the founders of the Faculty Scholarship Fund. Finegan died in 1974, and Finegan Hall, one of the school's dormitories, is named in his honor.

Rev. Bernard Russell taught mathematics at Gannon for 23 years until his unexpected death in February 1969. He was always ready to provide personal help for students and readily loaned books from his private collection, but not before writing "stolen from Bernard M. Russell" inside. The engineering building where he taught most of his classes was renamed Russell Hall in his honor.

Rev. Joseph E. Hipp joined the Gannon faculty upon his ordination in 1960. Unlike most priests, however, he did not enter religious life immediately after finishing school. After graduating from Strong Vincent High School in 1943, he joined the 54th Infantry Division under Gen. George Patton. Father Hipp landed on Omaha Beach in Normandy and fought in the Battle of the Bulge, earning two Purple Hearts and a Bronze Star. After the war, he worked as a news photographer and in advertising before entering the seminary. During his tenure as Gannon's financial aid officer, Father Hipp significantly expanded the grants, scholarships, and loans available to Gannon students. He was killed in a car accident in 1967 at just 42 years old.

The 1962 math and physics faculty are pictured here; from left to right are (first row) Rev. James McCullough, instructor in mathematics; James Freeman, director of mathematics; and Rev. Robert Sciamanda, instructor; (second row) Dean Kraus, dean of pure and applied science; Rev. Bernard Russell, associate professor of mathematics; and Mr. Weidle, instructor.

Mario Bagnoni was born in Sarzana, Italy, in 1922. After completing a successful 22-year career at the Erie Police Department, retiring as the deputy chief of detectives, he came to Gannon and founded the college's security department. He served as the security director for more than 20 years while also serving eight terms as a member of Erie's city council.

Jerry Kraus came to Cathedral College in 1937 after Monsignor Wehrle offered him $5 more than he was being paid by the Union Carbon and Carbide Company. Kraus taught physics and mathematics and eventually became the dean of the Division of Pure and Applied Science at Gannon College. He introduced electrical and mechanical engineering, industrial management, engineering technology, and the general science programs to the school and developed the layout for the Zurn Science building.

Sr. Doloretta Thorn was the second and longest-serving dean of Villa Maria College. One of six Sisters of St. Joseph on the school's faculty when it opened in 1925, she became acting dean in 1941 when Sr. Stella Harrington retired. Sister Doloretta was officially installed as dean and the executive officer of the college in 1943 and served in that position until her retirement in 1966.

The 1965 president's council included, from left to right, (first row) Dr. John Waldron, President Nash, and Gerald Kraus; (second row) Rev. John Slater, Dr. Joseph Scottino, Rev. Norbert G. Wolf, Msgr. Louis Lorei, Rev. Casimir Lubiak, Rev. Louis Puscas, and John Hynes. The council was the university's policy-making body and coordinated the activities of the academic departments. Its major policy decision for 1965 was eliminating theology and philosophy examinations as a condition for graduation.

The Religious Community of the Congregation of the Divine Spirit was founded by Bishop Gannon in 1956. The sisters were an active part of the Gannon community until the mid-1960s, serving many clerical functions across the campus. Their original motherhouse on West Sixth Street was eventually converted to a Gannon dormitory and residence for faculty priests. The sisters are still active today, teaching and ministering to the aged in Canton, Ohio.

Like many of Gannon's early instructors, John E. Waldron, pictured here in 1961, began teaching at Cathedral Prep. In 1936, Monsignor Wehrle asked him to take a teaching position at Cathedral College, where he taught Latin, history, and political science. He left Gannon twice during his career. The first was from 1942 to 1944, when he entered the military to serve as a cryptographer during World War II, and the second was in the late 1940s, to earn a doctorate in economics at the University of Pittsburgh. In 1950, he was appointed dean of the Division of Business Administration. For his distinguished service to the Catholic Church, Pope John XXIII awarded Dr. Waldron the Pro Ecclesia et Pontifice in 1963. The Waldron Campus Center, sometimes referred to as "the university's living room," bears his name.

As a diocesan college, theology and the Catholic intellectual tradition are fundamental to a Gannon education, making the theology faculty an important part of the Gannon community. Pictured here in the Wehrle Hall lobby is the 1962 theology faculty. From left to right are Revs. R. Sullivan, J. Peterson, J. Schanz, H. Niebling, and J. Hilbert.

Members of Gannon's 1967 English and education faculty are seen here; from left to right are Dr. John S. Rouch, Charles Smith, Joseph Gavin, Edward Babowicz, and John Young.

Bishop Edward McManaman was born in Wilkes-Barre, Pennsylvania, on May 3, 1900, and worked as a coal miner and newspaper reporter before entering the priesthood. He was a close advisor of Monsignor Wehrle and taught theology at Cathedral College from the year it opened. He served on numerous committees and boards related to Catholic education in the Erie diocese, including the first board of trustees for Gannon College, and led the campaign that raised $200,000 for the construction of Gannon's first library. He was appointed the rector of St. Peter's Cathedral in 1936 and the auxiliary bishop of the Erie diocese in 1948. Bishop McManaman is pictured here receiving an honorary doctorate degree from Archbishop Gannon in 1964, just a short time before his untimely death.

Dr. Joseph P. Scottino first came to Gannon in 1945 as a student. After receiving a PhD in political science from Fordham University, he returned to Gannon and began teaching in the political science department in 1955. He went on to serve as the director of the evening school, director of the graduate school, the college's first vice president for academic affairs, and provost before succeeding Monsignor Nash as Gannon's third president. Dr. Scottino's contributions to Gannon were innumerable and included establishing the physician's assistant program, evening and summer sessions, the liberal studies program, and the Gannon-Hahnemann family medicine program. He is best remembered, however, for overseeing the transition of Gannon College to Gannon University in 1979. Dr. Scottino retired in 1987.

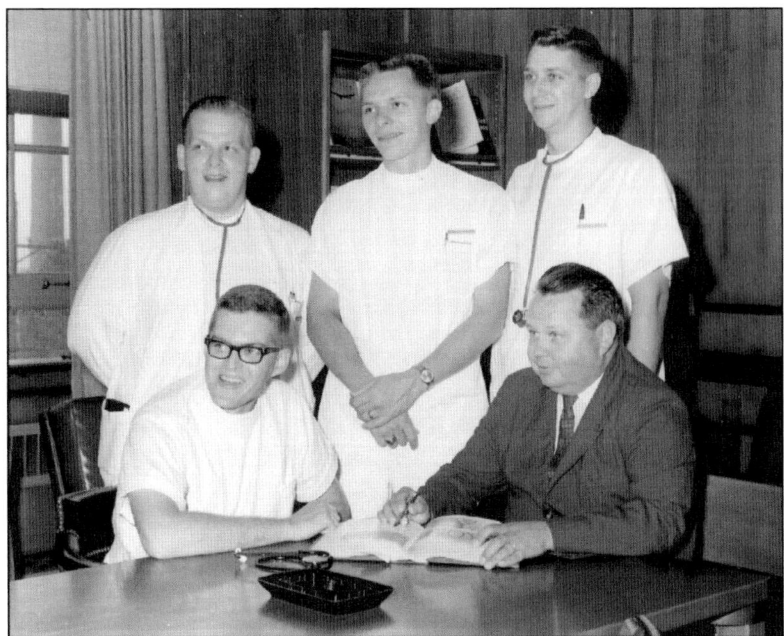

Dr. Elmer Kohlmiller, who retired in 1982, taught at Gannon for 26 years and chaired the biology department. He is pictured here in 1967 with four of his former students who went on to become physicians. Seated is Dr. David R. Jobes, and standing from left to right are Drs. Forrest C. Mischler, Ronald Zieziula, and William C. Wilhelm.

Dr. M. Daniel Henry served as Gannon's fourth president from 1987 to 1991. At his inauguration, he said, "Gannon isn't its buildings, as wonderful as they are. Gannon isn't its curriculum, as terrific as it is. Gannon is its people—its students, its faculty and staff, its trustees, its alumni, and its many, many friends." His most significant achievement as president was overseeing the integration of Gannon and Villa Maria Colleges.

Dr. Thomas Ostrowski, on the right, received his PhD in political science from the University of Houston. While in Texas, he taught and worked with inmates from prisons in Houston and Huntsville, Texas. A native of Erie, he began his Gannon career in 1976 as a professor of political science; over the next 40 years, he also served as the dean of humanities, vice president of academic affairs, and as interim president from 2000 to 2001. In addition to his long tenure at the university, he was also a consultant and speechwriter for Erie mayor Louis Tullio. Dr. Ostrowski taught up until his death in 2016. He is seen here with Nash Library's assistant director and archivist Bob Dobiesz selecting the winner of a set of encyclopedias.

Dr. Antoine M. Garibaldi served as Gannon's sixth president from 2001 to 2010. Garibaldi holds a PhD in educational psychology and is considered an expert in college retention for African American men. A native of New Orleans, he served as provost and chief academic officer of his alma mater, Howard University, and vice president for academic affairs at Xavier University before coming to Gannon. During his tenure as Gannon's president, enrollment increased by 24 percent to more than 4,200 students and the university's endowment more than doubled. He also oversaw the establishment of the Erie Technology Incubator, the construction and renovation of numerous campus buildings, and an expansion of the university to three colleges. Since leaving Gannon, Dr. Garibaldi has served as the president of the University of Detroit Mercy.

Msgr. David Rubino was ordained in the Diocese of Erie and began his teaching career, as many of Gannon's clergy faculty members, at Cathedral Preparatory High School. He was serving as Gannon's vice president for external affairs when he was appointed interim president in 1991 and then president in 1992. During his nine-year tenure as president, he oversaw the conversion of the former Carlisle's department store to the A.J. Palumbo Academic Center and the renovation of Beyer Hall, Zurn Science Center, and the Hammermill Center. The Waldron Campus Center was also constructed during his presidency. Today, he is the director of external affairs for the Lake Erie College of Osteopathic Medicine.

Gannon's current president, Dr. Keith Taylor, came to Gannon University in 2005 from Daemen College, where he was chair of the physical therapy department. He holds degrees in physical therapy and exercise science and a PhD in anatomy and cell biology. Taylor served as Gannon's provost and vice president of academic affairs until May 2011, when he was appointed the university's seventh president. During his tenure, Gannon has undergone significant growth in academic programs and its physical presence in Erie, and for the first time in its history, opened a branch campus in Ruskin, Florida. Community involvement has been a cornerstone of Taylor's presidency, as evidenced by the formation of the neighborhood revitalization programs Erie-GAINS (Gannon Alliance to Improve Neighborhood Sustainability) and Our West Bayfront, as well as the St. Joseph House of Faith in Action.

Rev. Robert J. Levis—chairman of the theology department, registrar, and the dean of liberal studies—is quoted as saying, "I stay at Gannon to do what I can to maintain the university's fidelity to Christ. He is the center of the whole place. He is the teacher in every classroom, the chairman of every department, the director of every program, the coach of every team, the chef of every meal."

"A teacher must equally balance a love of the discipline with a love of the students. If that becomes lopsided, the student suffers." This is how Dr. John S. Rouch described his educational philosophy in *Gannon Magazine*. He began teaching in the English department in 1959 and went on to serve as the graduate school dean for 15 years, retiring in 1991. He won numerous teaching awards, including the university's Distinguished Faculty Award.

Dr. Matti Moosa was born in Mosul, Iraq, in 1924. Before joining the Gannon faculty in 1966, Moosa served as an attorney and political analyst at the US embassy in Baghdad and as president of the Middle East Institute of Research. He is among the most published of Gannon professors and is especially well-known for numerous books on Middle Eastern history and culture. He received the Distinguished Faculty Award in 1988.

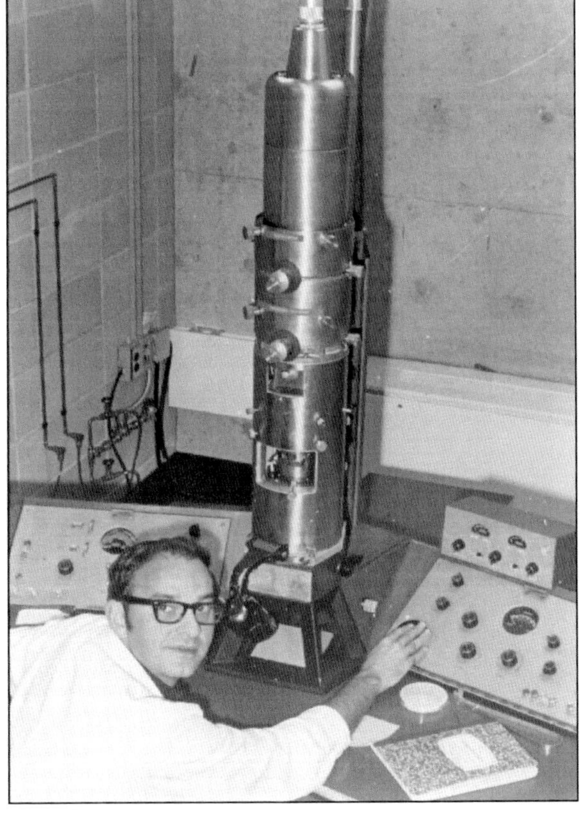

Rev. Joseph Gregorek has been an institution in Gannon's biology department for more than 42 years. Gregorek first started teaching at Gannon in 1965, the year he was ordained. In 2011, he was honored as a distinguished professor of biology. Gregorek has lectured at medical schools across Asia and is actively involved in medical ethics studies.

In the history of every university, there are a handful of people who become synonymous with the school and what it stands for. One of Gannon's most legendary figures was one of its maintenance men, Joe Luckey. He entered Gannon as a freshman in 1952 but never graduated due to lack of funds. He was beloved by the staff and students, most of whom Luckey claimed to know. Luckey was awarded the Archbishop Gannon Medal of Distinction for his service to the university. Today, one of the university's most coveted commencement awards is the Joe Luckey Service Award, which is given for "outstanding dedication and service to Gannon University." He was passionate about music, restoring pipe organs and endowing an annual concert series for the Erie Chamber Orchestra. Luckey passed away in 2011 at the age of 82.

Bishop Alfred M. Watson, seen here at Gannon's 1975 commencement, was a part of Gannon College history from the very beginning. He was in the first graduating class of Cathedral Preparatory School and was one of the young men Monsignor Wehrle sent to Villa Maria College when no other options were available. Bishop Watson went on to teach religion at Cathedral College; upon becoming bishop, he was appointed chairman of Gannon's board of trustees.

Robert Morosky graduated from Gannon in 1963 with a bachelor's degree in accounting. Morosky and his wife, Dianne, have been among Gannon's most significant benefactors, endowing a scholarship and making donations that enabled the Robert H. Morosky Academic Center. He is also a prolific artist whose paintings can be found in many campus buildings. Morosky was awarded the Gannon Medal of Distinction for his dedication to the university.

Bruce Morton Wright was a Gannon alumnus, the university's music director, an instructor of fine arts, and director of Gannon's concert band. One of his passions was introducing classical music to the Erie community by providing orchestra and opera performances free of charge. He did this by assembling 40 of the area's finest musicians as the director and conductor of the Erie Chamber Orchestra, which was based at the university.

One of Gannon's most significant benefactors was A.J. Palumbo. While Palumbo only had an eighth-grade education, he was a shrewd businessman and made his fortune in the coal, gas, and timber industries. His mission later in life was to share his wealth, especially with private colleges and universities. Palumbo served on Gannon's board of trustees, and the Palumbo Academic Center and A.J.'s Way bear his name. Palumbo passed away in 2002 at the age of 95.

Rev. Mai Thanh Phanh was born in North Vietnam in 1936. After escaping to France in 1954, he studied at universities in France and Rome before enrolling at Gannon in 1964. Eventually, he returned to Vietnam to teach at the University of Danang but fled again in 1975, this time in a small boat leading a group of refugees. They crossed the China Sea, enduring pirates and a typhoon, and landed in Guam, where he remained to help a thousand refugees find work and job training. In 1976, he returned to Gannon as a professor of theology but spent much of his free time helping to resettle Vietnamese refugees in Erie and Buffalo. In March 1979, he was recognized by the National Conference of Bishops: "In gratitude to Fr. Mai Thanh Phanh whose humanitarian efforts and selfless dedication in assisting and caring for refugees have demonstrated a commitment to the highest human values while promoting a new life, hope, and opportunity for Southeast Asian refugees." He died unexpectedly a year later at the age of 44.

Three

PLACES

The Gannon Arch first greeted students in the fall of 1999 and was built to commemorate the school's 75th anniversary. The arch, which spans West Seventh Street, was designed by WTW Architects of Pittsburgh, is 20 feet tall, and is the focal point of the campus. At its dedication, Erie mayor Joyce Savocchio observed that "they have outdone McDonald's with the arches."

On May 1, 1948, Gannon broke ground for its first athletic facility on the site of the Strong family's servants' quarters. Built at a cost of $500,000, the Gannon Auditorium—or "audi," as it was commonly called—was dedicated in January 1950. In addition to being home to the school's basketball, volleyball, and intramural teams for nearly 70 years, the auditorium has hosted hundreds of events and was considered the city of Erie's unofficial civic center before the Erie Civic Center was built. Ronald Reagan, John F. Kennedy, Richard Nixon, and Three Dog Night are just some of the luminaries who have appeared there. The auditorium was renamed the Hammermill Center in 1983 after the university received a generous donation from the paper company to renovate the center.

In 1959, Gannon purchased a former auto parts store at Sixth and French Streets. After extensive renovations, it dedicated the new Dale Hall on February 7, 1960. The building, which housed classrooms and the Reserve Officer Training Corps (ROTC) program, was named after Gannon alumnus Lt. Dale Hall. Hall was killed in action during the Korean War and awarded the Silver Star for heroism. The site where the building once stood is now occupied by Erie Insurance Group.

As Gannon College began to grow, finding housing for its clergy faculty was a challenge, so the school purchased a mansion from the Fredrick C. Jarecki family in 1950. It was home to many of Gannon's best-known faculty, including Gannon's second president, Monsignor Nash. The building was named the Barr Faculty House in 1972 after Rev. Joseph J. Barr, chairman of the social sciences and director of the political science department, who lived there for many years.

In Gannon's early years, finding student housing was a challenge. Students lived in private residences in the downtown area and even on one floor of the former Richford Hotel, which was located at Sixth and State Streets. To address the housing shortage, Gannon purchased the Lawrence Hotel Annex, located at 21 West Ninth street, for $345,000. The building had formerly been a part of one of Erie's landmarks: the opulent Lawrence Hotel. After the renovation, it was renamed South Hall and became home to 160 upperclassmen and some faculty members. Gannon sold the building in 1976; today, it is a senior living facility called Tullio Towers.

Gannon broke ground for its first new residence hall on October 9, 1956, on the former site of the Wallace home, which Gannon purchased in 1947. The dorm was financed by a 40-year government loan and cost approximately $700,000. When it opened in 1957, Wehrle Hall, which was named in honor of Gannon's first president, was filled to capacity with 240 students. For many years it was a men's dorm, but today is coed.

Our Lady of Victory watched over generations of Villa Maria College students, first at the Sisters of St. Joseph motherhouse in Erie and later at the A'Hearn Academic Building on the Millcreek Township campus. The statue represented the college's early history and its Catholic tradition.

After the 1989 merger of Villa Maria College and Gannon University, Villa's Millcreek Township campus continued to operate as Gannon's branch campus for several years. Eventually, the remaining academic programs and faculty relocated to Gannon's downtown Erie campus.

When Bishop Gannon purchased the Strong mansion, several additional support buildings were included, including a sizable building that was formerly the carriage house and stables. The building was renovated to house the university's first science labs. Downey Hall, named after Msgr. Thomas Downey, who was the pastor of St. Patrick's Church and a financial supporter of the Gannon School of Arts and Science, was also used in the 1970s as a student activity center and the black cultural center. The building is now part of the Waldron Student Center.

In December 1968, ground was broken for what would be the largest building on the Gannon campus. Sen. Hubert Humphrey, an honorary Gannon alumnus, was in Erie campaigning on that day and presented the groundbreaking shovel to Melvin Zurn, director of the Zurn Foundation, which supplied much of the funding for the building, as Monsignor Nash and Everett Zurn looked on. The Zurn Science Center doubled the number of classrooms and laboratories on campus. The first floor contained the physics department, the second floor was mechanical engineering, psychology was on the third floor, and chemistry was on the fourth. The building underwent significant renovation and modernization in 1998.

Unique among the university's dorms and housing facilities are Kenilworth Apartments, which were built in 1924. The apartments are among the most spacious on campus and have as many as four bedrooms each. No one is sure where the building's name came from, but an article in *Gannon Edge* magazine postulated that it might be named after Kenilworth Castle in Warwickshire, England, because of the many external design features they share.

In September 1988, Gannon president M. Daniel Henry presided over the dedication of three new student apartment buildings on Sassafras Street. Freeman Hall was named after mathematics professor James Freeman, Lubiak Hall after dean of humanities Fr. Casimir Lubiak, and Crispo Hall after Rev. Alphonse Crispo, who taught philosophy for 29 years.

One of the largest and most heavily used buildings on the Gannon campus is the Nash Library. Dedicated in 1973, the library was designed by Father Lubiak, Gannon 's librarian, and built at a cost of $4.2 million. The building also contained the Schuster Art Gallery and the campus TV station. The library was renamed in honor of Gannon president Monsignor Nash in 1977 upon his retirement. The library underwent a massive renovation in 2018 to make it more relevant for today's students, and it is now the most technologically advanced building on campus.

Beyer Hall was rededicated in 2016, a total of 56 years after it initially opened, with a new mission. Gone were the classrooms and laboratories; in their place, after a $6.3 million renovation, was a collaborative space where domestic and international students can work together and learn from one another. The 40,000-square-foot complex brings all of the university's student organizations, including the Student Government Association, Interfraternity and Panhellenic Councils, and Students Against Violence, under one roof. It also brings together the schools' international programs, such as the Robert and Suzanne Barker Globalization Institute and Global Enrollment and Engagement Division.

Gannon has a long history of repurposing downtown Erie buildings that have fallen into disrepair or are no longer in use. One example is the Palumbo Academic Center at the corner of Seventh and Peach Streets. The former Trask Department Store is now one of the busiest and most heavily used buildings on Gannon's campus. It is home to the campus bookstore; the Student Success Center; the College of Humanities, Education, and Social Services; and numerous classroom and offices.

Named after Gannon benefactor A.J. Palumbo, A.J.'s Way is a greenway that connects the northern and southern parts of campus. The landscaped brick walkway meanders through trees, wildflowers, bird feeders, benches, and a mural depicting Gannon history. The site was dedicated in 1999 and sits where Gannon's original mechanical engineering building and former campus post office once stood.

Members of Gannon's theater program christen the steps of Scottino Hall in 1994. Built in the 1920s as the Church of Christian Science, Gannon purchased the building in 1983. It was used by various departments and programs until the Schuster Theater moved in, in 1995. The theater hosts several student-led productions each year in addition to concerts, lectures, and other performances. The building also contains offices, classrooms, and scenic and costume shops.

Just outside of the Waldron Student Center is a circular group of benches, one of which includes a life-size statue of Jesus in conversation with two students. Jesus is holding a scroll inscribed with Matthew 5:14: "You are the light of the world. A town built on a hill cannot be hidden." One of the benches was donated by Dennis McConnell, a 1970 graduate, and is dedicated to his parents for their support while he was a Gannon student.

The 1950s were a time of rapid growth for the college. Among the major additions to the campus was the Engineering Building, which facilitated the rapid growth of Gannon's engineering programs. Completed in 1954, the building was designed by Gifford and Sunda Architects and contained two large lecture halls, five laboratories, offices, and classrooms. The building, which was renamed Russell Hall in honor of Rev. Bernard Russell, was torn down in 1998 to make room for the Waldron Student Center.

The Waldron Campus Center, which was dedicated on October 30, 1999, was designed by Williams-Trebilcock-Whitehead Architects. The 120,000-square-foot center conjoins Gannon's oldest and most historic buildings. By modernizing and bringing Downey Hall, Beyer Hall, Old Main, and the Hammermill Center under one roof, the center has become the focal point of campus life.

Located where Gannon's original theater once stood, Friendship Green is an oasis in the middle of the Gannon campus. Owned by the Cathedral of St. Paul of the Episcopal Diocese of Northwest Pennsylvania, the green is used for many school-sponsored activities including fundraisers, recruitment fairs, Greek events, and freshmen orientation. It is a favorite lunch spot for students grabbing a bite from the adjacent Waldron Center.

Prior to 1959, Gannon's ROTC program was located in Aquinas Hall, at the corner of Sixth and Sassafras Streets. Gannon purchased the former home of steamboat operator Thomas Carter in 1947. After the ROTC program moved to Dale Hall, the building became a faculty residence and small chapel before becoming the college's Health Center in the 1960s and 1970s.

Gannon's current bookstore, which is in the Palumbo Academic Center, is a large, bright, welcoming retail store that sells clothing, college-branded merchandise, and more in addition to books. It was not always that way, as can be seen in this photograph of Gannon's bookstore in 1977. The store, which was located in the Walker Building, was small, cramped, and sold only books and school supplies. Today, the Walker Building contains student apartments.

The Sisters of St. Joseph founded Villa Maria elementary school, Villa Maria Academy high school, and Villa Maria College all at their motherhouse in Erie. Recognizing that one day they would have to find a new location for the schools, they purchased Maryvale, the former Reed estate in Millcreek Township. This is one of the original buildings, which the sisters operated for many years as Maryvale kindergarten.

Gannon opened its first women's dorm in 1972. Prior to this, female students were housed at the former Hamot Nursing School Dormitory on lower State Street. When it first opened, the east wing, which was originally called North Hall, was occupied by female students, while the west wing was occupied by male students. Eventually, the entire dorm became women only. Today, Finegan Hall, which was renamed in honor of Owen Finegan, the dean of pure and applied sciences, in 1975, is again co-ed.

Gannon's location just blocks away from Presque Isle Bay and Lake Erie makes it a perfect place to study freshwater biology. For the past 20 years, that opportunity has been significantly enhanced by the school's research vessel, the *Environaut*. Built in 1950 as a fishing boat, the vessel is now equipped with sonar, an underwater camera, and an onboard scientific laboratory.

The Robert H. Morosky Academic Center is home to the Morosky College of Health Professions and Sciences. The 100,000-square-foot building, which originally housed Verizon's regional headquarters, contains laboratories, classrooms, offices, a café, and a sunken outdoor courtyard. The building opened in 2008 and has the region's largest patient simulation center, which includes an emergency room, operating room, critical care unit, and labor/delivery suite.

In 1981, Gannon purchased the First Presbyterian Church located at Fifth and Peach Streets when the congregation merged with the Presbyterian Church of the Covenant. The church was rebuilt in 1950 after a fire destroyed most of the original church complex, which was built in 1860. Today, it is Gannon's Mary Seat of Wisdom Chapel and features stained-glass windows designed by Erie artist John Vahanian. Attached to the chapel is Gannon's human resources department.

Gannon bought the former Boys and Girls Club of Erie in 2001 and converted it into the Erie Technology Incubator. Built in 1925 as Erie's original YMCA, today the building is Gannon's Advanced Engineering Center, which houses the school's mechanical, biomedical, and industrial engineering programs.

Gannon has owned several of the homes located along millionaires' row on West Sixth Street. Among them is the mansion built by Erie industrialist George I. Black. From 1963 to 2012, the mansion was home to Gannon's Tau Kappa Epsilon fraternity. In 2014, the building became Gannon's Forensic Investigation Center. The center allows students to learn forensic principles using the center's interrogation room, crime scene reenactment areas, forensic lab, and a firearms training simulator.

Gannon's Center for Business Ingenuity opened in 2015 in the former Kresge Department Store. Located at 900 State Street, the 60,000-square-foot building is home to the Dahlkemper School of Business, the Erie Technology Incubator, and the Small Business Development Center. Housing all three organizations allows for unique collaborative opportunities between students, faculty, entrepreneurs, and business consultants. In addition to classrooms and offices, the center also contains the school's Business Information Systems Laboratory.

Gannon has been an integral part of the downtown Erie community for more than 70 years and today is one of the city's largest employers and landowners. Over the past several years, it has been especially active in community efforts to help revive the west bay-front area where the school is located. One example of its commitment is the St. Joseph House of Faith in Action. The 2,400-square-foot house was built by Gannon students, faculty, and community members and serves as the outreach center for Gannon's Center for Social Concerns. It provides a community gathering space as well as overnight accommodations for students and groups doing community service in the area.

In August 2015, Gannon opened its first campus outside of Erie in Ruskin, Florida. Located in Hillsborough County between Tampa and Bradenton, the university leased commercial office space and in its first year enrolled 22 students in the doctor of physical therapy program. At the time, it was one of only six universities in the country offering the degree. Within the next few years, it added programs in occupational therapy, athletic training, and sport and exercise medicine; by 2018, a total of 120 students were enrolled. With the rapidly expanding student body and more academic programs coming online, the university purchased the building and surrounding property and began a major expansion of the campus in 2018.

Gannon's Center for Communication and the Arts occupies the former Loyal Christian Benefit Association headquarters at the corner of Seventh and Peach Streets. It is home to the campus radio station, WERG, the *Gannon Knight* newspaper, Collins Institute for Archaeological Research, Schuster Gallery, and the School of Communication and the Arts.

In 2017, Judith Alstadt donated 3.57 acres of land on Brokenstraw Creek in Warren County to the university for use as an environmental research center. She and her husband, Donald, who was a renowned chemist and chairman of Lord Corporation, built two lodges on the property in 1968 as their country retreat. The research center allows environmental science and biology students to live on-site as they study the wide variety of ecosystems found there.

Four

Campus Life

A highlight of the spring semester is the annual Founder's Day Convocation. Pictured here in 1966, students who have excelled in their academic field, those who have shown exceptional service to campus organizations and causes, and student organizations are recognized for their achievements and contributions to the university.

GANNON
ROTC
COLLEGE

Gannon has had an ROTC program since 1948. Until 1954, the program was a military police corps unit, but since then it has focused on general military science. Participation was mandatory for all male students until 1969, when the student body and the theology department convinced the administration that participation should be voluntary. In 1957, when this photograph was taken, cadets were instructed in arms, tactics, supply, and administration and participated in weekly marching drills. Today, Gannon is the host school for the Pride of Pennsylvania battalion, which also includes Mercyhurst University and Penn State Behrend.

Gannon's ROTC drill team marches down State Street in the 1956 Christmas parade. The team, which often appeared in parades and exhibitions, impressed the crowd of 100,000 people, winning the award for best precision marching unit and taking home the $50 prize.

In 1958, Gannon's ROTC program established a chapter of the National Society of Scabbard and Blade, a military honor society. Members worked to improve their leadership skills and raise the standards of military education in American colleges. The society sponsored the Military Ball, Gannon's only formal dance, in honor of the ROTC program's senior members.

At one time, Erie's four Catholic colleges—Gannon, Villa Maria, Mercyhurst, and the Saint Vincent Nursing School—had very close social ties. Since Gannon was all men and the other schools all women, the schools frequently participated in each other's dances and social events. There was even an intercollegiate board, pictured here in 1961. The board held its own social events, such as the glee club singalong seen below, and was responsible for the maintenance and upkeep of the student union house, which was located on West Sixth Street. The close ties between the schools began to fade after Gannon and Mercyhurst became coed in the 1960s.

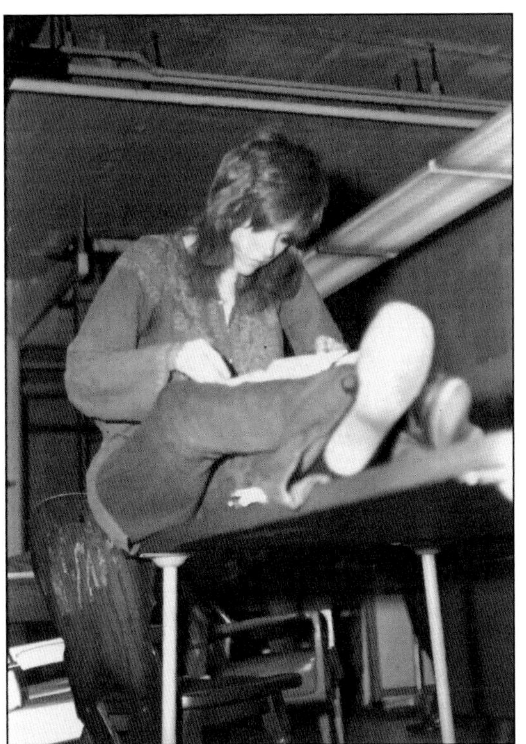

The St. Thomas More Club invited Jane Fonda and political activist Tom Hayden to speak at Gannon in 1972. Fonda and Hayden were touring the country as part of the Indochina peace campaign and presented a lecture and slideshow of Fonda's trip to North Vietnam to a standing-room-only crowd in Zurn Science Center.

On October 15, 1969, about 200 Gannon students joined 100 Mercyhurst students as they marched from their campus to Perry Square. There they joined 500 others, including members of the Black Panther Party, to participate in the Erie Vietnam Moratorium Day. Gannon theology professor Rev. Richard Sullivan was the opening speaker, and a tree was planted in honor of the 38,000 Americans who had died in the war.

On March 3, 1970, about 400 students marched into Monsignor Nash's office with a list of proposals developed by the student senate that they felt would improve student life but were not being taken seriously by the administration. They occupied the first floor of Old Main until Nash arrived and listened to their concerns, which included instituting a pass-fail program and converting Downey Hall into a student-run student union. According to the *Gannon Knight*, it was a polite crowd, and the sit-in only lasted 40 minutes.

The 1971–1972 student handbook contained anything a student could possibly want to know about life on the Gannon campus, from academic information to the year's social calendar. It also contained this admonition, probably in response to the protests that had occurred on campus the year before, "At least take the time to read the academic policies as well as the chapter on campus discipline. Ignorance of regulations is not an acceptable excuse in any society."

The staff of the *Lance*, Gannon's yearbook, is hard at work in 1958. The first issue, which was published in 1952, was a relatively small memory book, but in the following year, it was expanded to document all facets of Gannon life. All of the Gannon yearbooks, as well as the Villa Maria yearbooks, were digitized by the Nash Library archives and can be viewed online. Most of the photographs in this book came from the *Lance*.

Vice President Hubert Humphrey was Gannon's 1966 convocation speaker. Accompanied by a security entourage of 50 people, he delivered a talk that focused on water pollution in Lake Erie and the need for colleges to be more involved in shaping their community's future. At the conclusion of his remarks, he was awarded an honorary doctorate degree from the college.

Vice presidential candidate Edmund Muskie, a senator from Maine, made a campaign appearance on the Gannon campus just days before the 1968 election. After attending Mass at St. Peter's Cathedral, he spoke to a large crowd in the Gannon auditorium. It would be the last time he visited the college since he and his running mate, Hubert Humphrey, lost the election to Richard Nixon and Spiro Agnew.

Delta Sigma Phi was founded in 1899 at the City College of New York and was the first fraternity to admit members without consideration of race or creed. Gannon's Gamma Rho chapter was chartered in 1954, making it Gannon's first fraternity. The fraternity is pictured here in 1960 with its chaplain, Father Yehl.

Potential pledges attend a rush party for Tau Kappa Epsilon in 1959. The fraternity, one of the largest in the world, was formed in 1899 at Illinois Wesleyan University. Gannon's Delta Chi chapter was chartered in 1955. Their motto is "Not for wealth, rank, or honor, but for personal worth and character."

Alpha Phi Delta was established in 1914 at Syracuse University as an Italian heritage fraternity. Gannon's Beta Rho chapter, pictured here in 1961, was formed in 1959 and held several annual events, including a Christmas party for the orphans of St. Joseph's home and a spaghetti dinner at St. Paul's church.

Lambda Iota Tau was an international honor society for English and foreign literature whose mission was to recognize and promote excellence in the study of literature in all languages. In 1961, Gannon's Alpha Nu chapter, pictured here with its advisors Dr. Rouch and Dr. Rowland, sponsored a campus series of motion pictures based on famous novels.

Gannon's radio station, WERG, began broadcasting from the basement of the Nash Library in 1972 using a 10-watt transmitter. The station, which is student managed and operated, has grown significantly over the years and moved several times. Today, it broadcasts with a 3,000-watt transmitter and is housed in the Center for Communication and the Arts. In 2014, it was voted the Best College Station in the Nation by the Intercollegiate Broadcasting System.

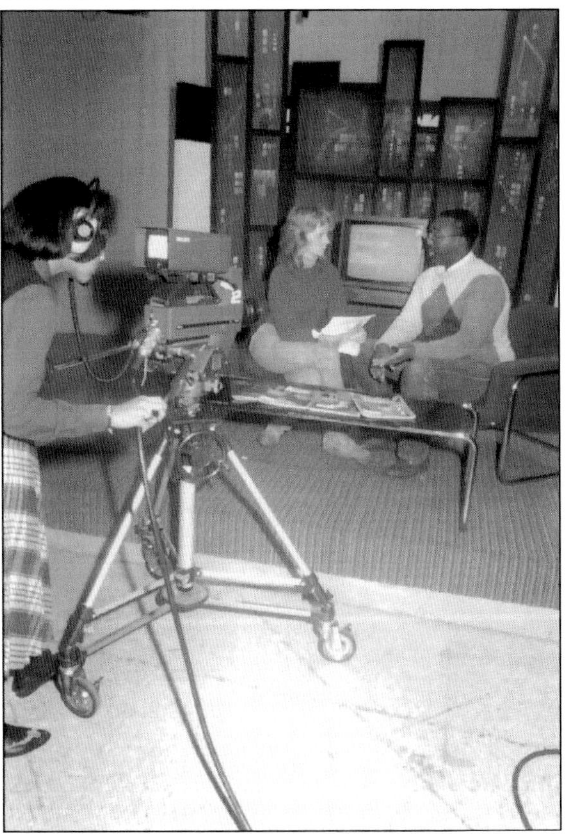

In 1984, the Federal Communications Commission granted a license to Gannon University Broadcasting to operate a television station, WETG Channel 66. The station was located in the basement of Nash Library and run by students and faculty in the theater and communications arts program. The station was an alternative to local stations and ran educational, entertainment, and Catholic programming. In 1988, it became a Fox affiliate and was sold in 1995.

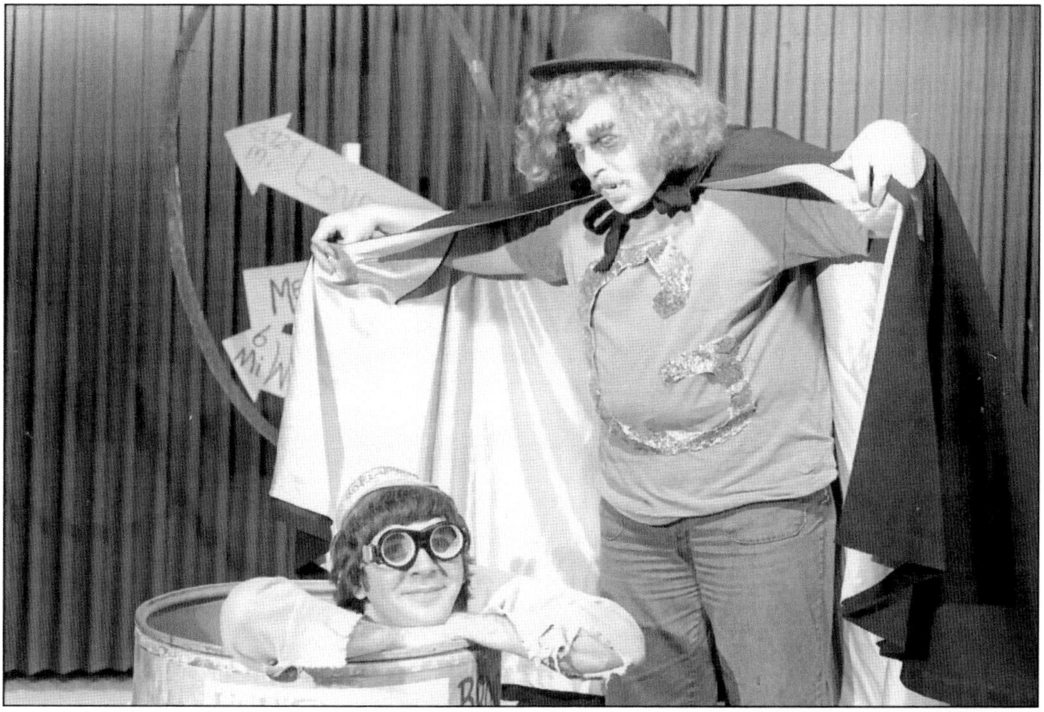

The TV & Radio Guild, an honor club for communications arts students, was formed in 1976. Members were expected to direct, produce, and present their own shows. One of the shows presented in that first year was a comedy entitled *Saturday Night Dead*. It starred Prof. A.J. Micelli as Igor (left) and Steve Bohen (right), a future Gannon faculty member, as Ghoulini.

Members of Alpha Psi Omega, the national honorary theater fraternity, pose for their official 1968 yearbook photograph in front of the former Gannon College Theater. The Gannon chapter was formed in 1960 and is still active on campus today. The site where this photograph was taken is now Friendship Green.

The Talisman Players were theater students who produced and performed plays in the Gannon College Theater. One of the four productions they put on in 1977 was *There is no Tragedy in Thebes*.

For many years, the Gannon auditorium was the largest public meeting place in Erie and at times was pressed into service on short notice. On September 13, 1960, Henry Cabot Lodge, Richard Nixon's vice presidential running mate, came to Erie to campaign. The rally was supposed to be held in Perry Square, but due to bad weather, it was moved into the auditorium, where 7,000 people listened to Lodge make the case for Nixon as president.

Students man the phones during Gannon's annual Phone-a-Thon in 1980. One of the school's primary fundraisers, students call alumni, family, and friends of the university soliciting donations, and in the process, they earn a salary and learn about philanthropy. After a 10-year hiatus, the student-run Phone-a-Thon returned in 2017.

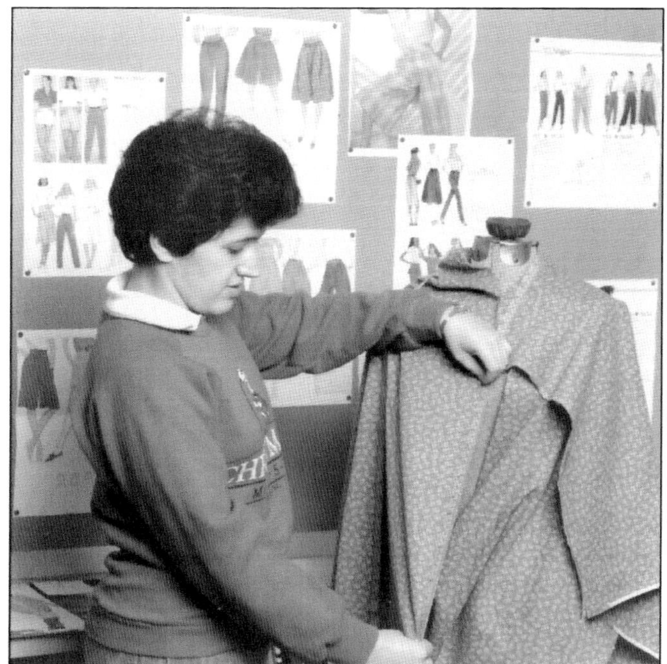

While Villa Maria College was probably best known for its nursing program, it offered 30 majors, including home economics. Students in this major took courses ranging from business and education to psychology and nutrition. The program allowed the students to focus on one of three concentrations: general home economics, home economics education, or merchandising and retailing.

Since the 1950s, concerts have been a regular part of Gannon life. The auditorium has seen performers from the early days of rock and roll, like the Lettermen and Four Tops, and bands from the 1960s, including Sly and the Family Stone and Gary Puckett & the Union Gap. The 1970s saw bands like Three Dog Night, Todd Rundgren, and Genesis. The concerts are always sponsored by a campus organization. In November 1974, the student union sponsored Frank Zappa and the Mothers of Invention (above). Unfortunately, the concert did not get good reviews, and the *Gannon Knight* referred to it as "one of the major disappointments of all time." In 1976, Hall and Oates (left) performed in the auditorium, sponsored by the Alpha Phi Delta fraternity, and received much better reviews.

Erie's waterfront has always held a special place in the hearts of Gannon students. These students are relaxing in front of the SS *North American* in 1964. The steamship, which ferried passengers from Erie to Port Dover, Ontario, during 1963, was a fixture at the public dock, which is today known as Dobbin's Landing, until 1967.

Gannon's Fall Frenzy, held on the first weekend of September, was a street fair that took place on Seventh Street, which was blocked off to traffic. The student government association–sponsored event included concerts, a volleyball tournament, and in 1985, the opportunity to smash an AMC Pacer with a sledgehammer.

Gannon's Blue Key honor society (above) was open to any junior or senior who had a high grade average and exhibited leadership in campus organizations. It hosted concerts and other events but was most known for the winter carnival, which began in 1956. The three-day carnival featured a talent show, art sale, car raffle, and the crowning of a queen. The 1964 winter carnival (below) was the first time a student from Gannon was among the candidates, joining young women from Mercyhurst, Villa Maria, the Saint Vincent College of Nursing, and the Hamot School of Nursing.

A highlight of Gannon's fall calendar is homecoming weekend. In addition to the football game and tailgating, events include the Alumni Association Distinguished Alumni Dinner, Villa Maria Alumnae High Tea, Circles of Distinction reception, and other events. Prior to 2017 it also included a homecoming parade, such as the one seen here in 1972 led by both Gannon's official mascot, the Gannon Knight, and its unofficial mascot at that time, Gumby.

Members of the Black Student Union relax in their Downey Hall lounge in 1974. According to the *Lance* yearbook, "The T.V. room, with vinyl and chrome furniture and shag carpeting looked especially impressive." The Union is still active today educating the Gannon community about African-American culture and history and helping to recruit and retain minority students.

The Gannon Wireless Society operated a ham radio station from a small room on the first floor of the Zurn Science Center. When they were broadcasting, the signal would occasionally be picked up by the language lab, disrupting the class. The club is pictured here in 1981 on the roof of the Zurn Science Center, where they had installed microwave antennas acquired from a local TV station.

Gov. Richard Thornburgh, who was in his second term as Pennsylvania's chief executive, was the 1985 commencement speaker. He was awarded an honorary degree of doctor of law and is seen here being hooded by Gannon's president Dr. Joseph Scottino and Bishop Michael Murphy. Six years earlier, Thornburgh had visited the campus to make the official announcement that Gannon had been granted university status.

Gannon has a very active student government association, as seen here in 1977. Comprised of class representatives and representatives of campus organizations, the association functions as the voice of the student body to faculty, staff, and administration. Student government also sponsors many campus-wide events, from social gatherings to lectures and concerts.

Gannon's Model UN, pictured here in 1978, was founded in 1954 by Fr. Joseph Barr, chair of the political science department. The program gives high school students the opportunity to learn about world issues and gain experience in leadership and debate. Gannon students act as advisors, moderators, and guides to the participants. What began as a program for Erie-area high schools today includes 800 students from Ohio, Pennsylvania, New York, and Canada.

Since 1994, biology professors Dr. Steve Ropski and Dave Gustafson have been leading a summer field course to Yellowstone National Park. Among the most popular of the university's travel classes, more than 350 students have spent a portion of their summer in the park earning credits while also whitewater rafting, horseback riding, and studying the wildlife and geology of the park.

Villa Maria College began offering nursing courses during World War II, and its collegiate nursing program was approved by the Pennsylvania State Board of Nurse Examiners in 1953. By the 1980s, when this photograph was taken, nursing was one of the college's largest majors, and the program was highly regarded. The Villa Maria School of Nursing still exists today and is a part of Gannon's Morosky College of Health Professions and Sciences.

In 2018, Gannon president Dr. Keith Taylor and Dr. Walter Iwanenko, vice president of academic affairs, announced the formation of I-HACK, the Institute for Health and Cyber Knowledge. The institute is located in the Knight Tower and includes a cybersecurity lab, a security-controlled hacking lab, and cyber defense lab. With the opening of the institute, the university began offering degrees in cyber engineering and cybersecurity.

One Saturday each fall, Gannon students in Erie and alumni around the country participate in Gannon's Invitation to Volunteer Everywhere, better known as GIVE Day. Laura Goble, director of the university's Center for Social Concerns, which sponsors the event, says "GIVE Day provides us the opportunity to serve, build community and live our mission with our neighbors." These students were among the 1,100 faculty, staff, students, and alumni who participated in 2014.

On August 25, 2018, Gannon's Ruskin, Florida, campus graduated its first class. Three years after the campus opened, 21 students from 11 states received their doctorate in occupational therapy. When Gannon opened the program in 2015, it was one of only six universities in the United States offering the degree. By 2018, the Florida campus was also offering graduate degrees in physical therapy, athletic training, and sport and exercise science.

Greeting fans and competitors at the entrance of McConnell Family Stadium is an eight-foot-tall bronze statue of the Gannon Golden Knight. The sculpture was created by Jon Hair, pictured here between student government association president Angela Coustillac and Gannon president Keith Taylor. Hair has created more than 50 monumental statues around the world, including 35 at colleges and universities.

Five

ATHLETICS

Gannon's top three scorers display their point totals for the 1955–1956 basketball season. From left to right are Dick Fox, Bob Vilchinsky, and Bill Jowett. Fox went on to serve as Gannon's first varsity baseball coach from 1958 until 1961. He returned to Gannon in 1978, coaching the Golden Knights basketball team until 1984, and then again for part of the 1995 season, ending his coaching career with a record of 100-58.

Gannon fielded its first football team in 1949 with Lou Tullio, the college's athletic director, as head coach and Jack Komora as his assistant. In its inaugural season, the team was undefeated and outscored its opponents 184-20, thanks in part to Art Arkelian, who scored touchdowns as a halfback, punt returner, and kickoff returner. The following year, the team had a difficult time finding opponents either because the schools they had played the year before discontinued their football programs or declined to play Gannon. The 1950 team finished 6-2 but would not play together again because the college could not financially support the team. Football would not return to Gannon until 1989. The 1949 team was inducted into the Athletics Hall of Fame in 1983.

Gannon's 1961–1962 men's basketball team is a legend in Gannon sports. It was the first basketball team from the college to make it to the NCAA Division II tournament, defeating nationally ranked teams along the way, including Tennessee A&I and Texas Southern. The team was coached by three former Gannon players. George Hesch, class of 1955, was the head coach, and his classmate Howard "Bud" Elwell and Dick Fox, class of 1958, were assistant coaches. Elwell also coached the golf and cross-country teams and served as the college's athletics director for more than 20 years. The team was inducted into Gannon's Athletics Hall of Fame in 2012, and coaches Hesch and Elwell, along with four of the players—Willie Alford, Jack Byrnes, Al Lawson, and Joe Gaeta—were also inducted for their individual accomplishments.

Nicknamed the "Little General" because of his leadership skills, Joe Gaeta played both basketball and baseball while at Gannon. Seen here while co-captain of the 1961–1962 basketball team, Gaeta was inducted into the Athletics Hall of Fame in 2011 and into the Pride of Pennsylvania ROTC Hall of Fame in 2017. Gaeta is also one of the co-founders of the university's Golden Knights Booster Club, which has raised hundreds of thousands of dollars to support the university's intercollegiate teams.

Gannon had an intercollegiate fencing team from the late 1950s until the 1960s. The team's coach was Laszlo Doemeny, who was also a physical education instructor and the school's intramural director. Before coming to Gannon, Doemeny was a freedom fighter during the Hungarian Revolution.

Gannon has had cheerleaders since the 1950s. Not to be confused with the school's competitive cheer team, cheerleaders have been a fixture at basketball games in the auditorium and at football games at McConnell Family Stadium. In 1961, when this photograph was taken, the women on the squad came from Mercyhurst College, which was an all-girls school at the time. No women from Villa Maria College participated because their administration would not approve it.

Gannon's bowling team won the National Association of Intercollegiate Athletics' (NAIA) first National Bowling Championship by defeating Central Oklahoma by 59 pins. The team, which was inducted into the Athletics Hall of Fame in 2011, was coached by Al Kendziora, who graduated from Gannon that year. The team was ranked number one by the NAIA out of 460 teams.

The 1955 golf team finished its season with a 5-2 record, defeating teams from Edinboro College, Youngstown State, and Behrend Center. They were ranked sixth out of 13 teams that competed in the Western Pennsylvania Small College Tourney. The team was coached by Fr. Gilio Dipre, a Gannon alumnus who taught philosophy at Gannon from 1955 to 1998.

Msgr. Addison Yehl taught at Gannon for 55 years and served as the chemistry department chair from 1951–2006. He was also a gifted tennis player and coached men's tennis, including this team from 1957. The ballroom in the Waldron Center is named in his honor.

As part of freshman orientation, Gannon hosted sports night, seen here in 1959. The evening pitted the athletic talents of the freshman class against those of the sophomore class. The evening began with a basketball game. At halftime, the classes competed in relay races, wrestling, and tug-of-war. Freshmen not competing in one of the events were required to be a part of the cheering section.

Dr. George Hesch was a legend at Gannon in both sports and teaching. He was the first Gannon basketball player to score 1,000 career points and was the team's leading scorer during the 1953 and 1954 seasons. He also coached the team from 1961 to 1963, taking the Knights to their first-ever NCAA tournament in 1962. In light of this and his coaching accomplishments, his jersey was retired, and he was elected to the Athletics Hall of Fame. Hesch was also a chemistry professor for 48 years, retiring in 2003.

Villa Maria College fielded teams in four sports: basketball, tennis, volleyball, and softball. The Villa Victors were a part of the Western Keystone Conference and competed with teams that included Gannon, Mercyhurst College, Allegheny College, branch campuses of the University of Pittsburgh and Penn State University, and other small private colleges. The 1984 softball team, below, played a short season of only eight games, but whether they had a winning or losing record is lost to history. The basketball team from the 1980s, seen above, had a significantly longer season, but due to a number of uncontrollable factors, the school did not field a team during the 1982 season.

Mel Witherspoon transferred to Gannon from Scottsbluff Community College in his junior year. For the next two years, he was captain of the basketball team and averaged more than 11 points and 11 rebounds per game. By the time he graduated in 1964, he had scored 537 points and made 522 rebounds. Witherspoon, who is now an Erie city councilman, was inducted into the Gannon Athletics Hall of Fame in 2017.

The 1966-1967 season was an eventful one for Gannon's men's basketball team. After finishing the season with a 20-3 record, it received a bid for an NCAA post-season tournament. Unbeknownst to the players, coaches, and president Monsignor Nash, Father Somers, the dean of students, told the NCAA that Gannon did not want to participate. That decision led to protests by the student body, pictured here with former star player Mel Witherspoon at center.

Gannon's 1986–1987 men's basketball team is the only one to have played in the NCAA Division II championship game, losing to Kentucky Wesleyan. The team played to capacity crowds in the Hammermill Auditorium all season, finishing with a record of 28-6, and also hosted the quarterfinals of the NCAA tournament.

Bob "Whitey" Dukiet was born in 1948 in New Jersey, where he was a high school basketball All-American. He went on to play for Bob Cousy at Boston College and was drafted by the Los Angeles Lakers. Before becoming Gannon's men's basketball coach, he coached at several other schools including Dartmouth College and Princeton University. During his coaching tenure at Gannon from 1989 to 1996, he amassed a record of 136-67 and took the team to the NCAA Division II national tournament four times.

In 1988, Gannon opened a much-needed recreation center on Peach Street just a couple blocks from Old Main. Constructed at a cost of $3.5 million, the center contained a gym, indoor running track, pool, physical fitness center, locker room, handball and racquetball courts, and offices for the athletics department. In 2014, the center underwent a $14.5 million modernization and expansion. Covering an entire city block, the new building includes a human-performance lab for use by physical therapy, occupational therapy, and exercise science students, as well as an indoor fieldhouse that allows year-round practice for sports such as soccer and football.

Erie mayor Louis J. Tullio was inducted into Gannon's Athletics Hall of Fame in 1983. He served as Gannon's head football coach from 1949 to 1950, head basketball coach from 1951 to 1956, and athletic director from 1949 to 1956. He is seen here with his wife, Grace, and Gannon president Dr. M. Daniel Henry at a ceremony establishing the Tullio Scholarship Fund.

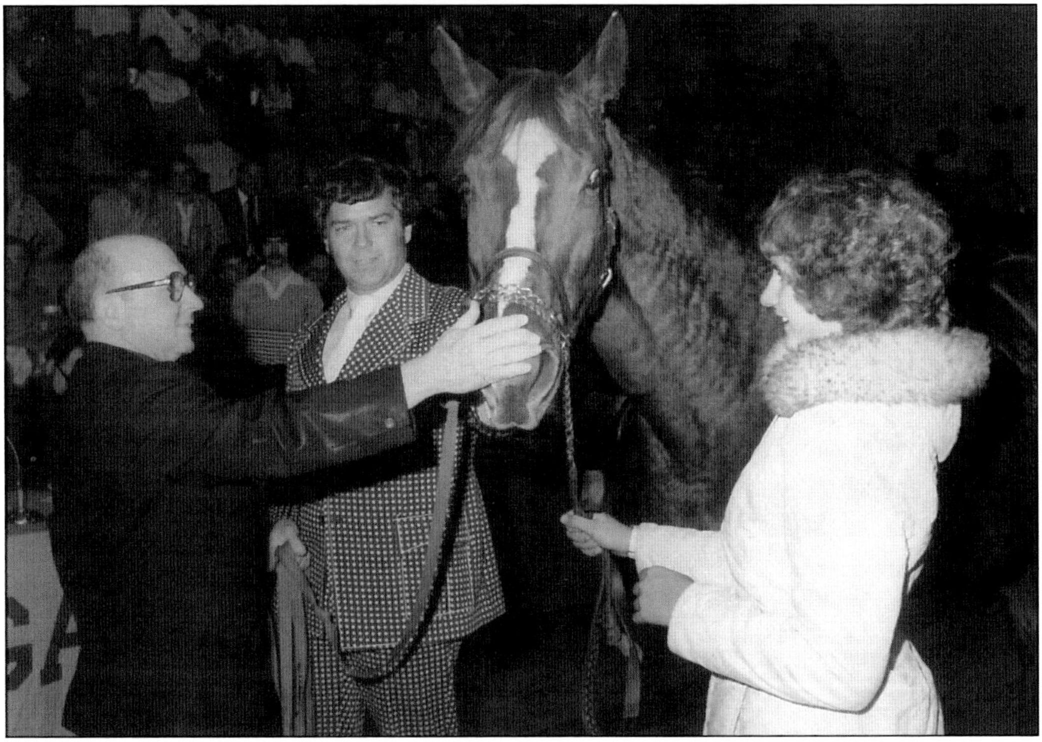

Gannon president Monsignor Nash grew up loving horses and was the proud owner of two Arabians, which he kept at his brother's farm in nearby Fairview, Pennsylvania. It was this passion that led to what is likely the most unusual spectacle ever at a Gannon basketball game. In April 1977, at a home game against Slippery Rock College, Nash was presented with a horse at center court as a retirement gift.

Organized women's sports came to Gannon in 1975. In addition to the softball team seen here, volleyball, basketball, and tennis teams were also started. The teams had no budget, so students were recruited not only to play but also to coach. The following year saw dedicated budgets that allowed the teams to pay coaches, buy uniforms, and travel to games.

Gannon has fielded a cross-country team since 1948, making it one of the college's longest-running sports. The 1966–1967 team pictured here finished the season with a 10-2 dual meet record. They finished in second place at the NAIA District 18 meet, losing to Pitt 40-15.

Pictured here at Ainsworth Field is the 1983 baseball team. The 3,000-seat minor league stadium was Gannon's home field until McConnell Family Stadium was built. Two of this team's members are still at Gannon. Joe Dolak is an assistant softball coach, and Mark Gaeta is the coordinator of capital support and athletics in the university advancement office. The team's pitcher, Scott Tarasovitch, went on to play professionally for the Erie Cardinals.

Women's basketball coach Judy Sauer, pictured here in her first year at Gannon with the 1985–1986 team, was inducted into the Athletics Hall of Fame in 2011. Over her five years coaching at Gannon, she had an 88-47 record and was named the Mideast Collegiate Conference Coach of the year in 1988. In that same year, she took the team to its first-ever NCAA tournament appearance, where it lost to Army.

Gannon's 1985 men's soccer team was one of the most talented teams in Gannon history. For the second year in a row, they won a bid to the NCAA Division II playoffs and finished the season 20-1. Coach Rob Russo, who entered the Gannon Athletics Hall of Fame in 2010, was named the 1985 Division II coach of the year. Also inducted into the Hall of Fame in 2010 were two of the players, Gerry van DeMerwe and Rob van Rheenen, both of whom were also All-Americans.

Gannon's club hockey team was formed in 1970 and played at the Glenwood Ice Rink, which was home to the semiprofessional Erie Lions hockey team. Today, the team is a member of the Upstate New York Club Hockey League and plays its home games in the Erie Insurance Arena against teams that include the University of Buffalo, Syracuse University, and hometown rival Mercyhurst University.

Members of the Gannon rifle team practice in 1956. The team, which was composed of marksmen from the ROTC program, was a member of the Lake Erie Intercollegiate Rifle Conference and competed against teams including Duquesne, Kent State, and John Carroll Universities. The team was unbeaten in 1971 and won the conference title.

Gannon's 1986 men's swimming team wrapped up its season by competing in the Penn-Ohio Conference Championship in Cleveland, Ohio. Under coach Greg Lampe, they finished seventh and set Gannon records in almost every event.

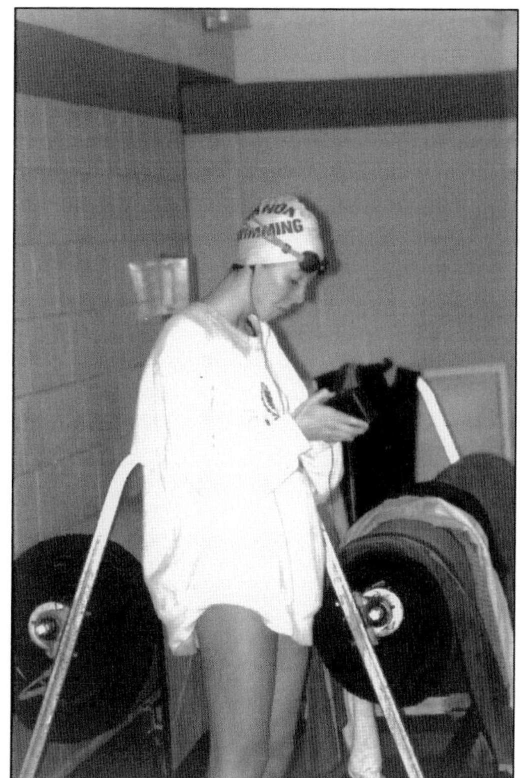

Sharon Crotzer Johnson is considered the best women's swimmer in Gannon history. She was named an All-American seven times while at Gannon and is the only Gannon swimmer ever to earn All-American status in all four years as an undergraduate. The 1995 graduate was inducted into the Gannon Athletics Hall of Fame in 2013.

Like many sports, women's soccer at Gannon began as a club sport in 1986. It did not take long, however, for the team to achieve varsity status. In 1987, they began competing in NCAA Division III, although most of the teams they played that year were Division II schools. By the time, this 1992–1993 team took to the field, Gannon had moved up to Division II.

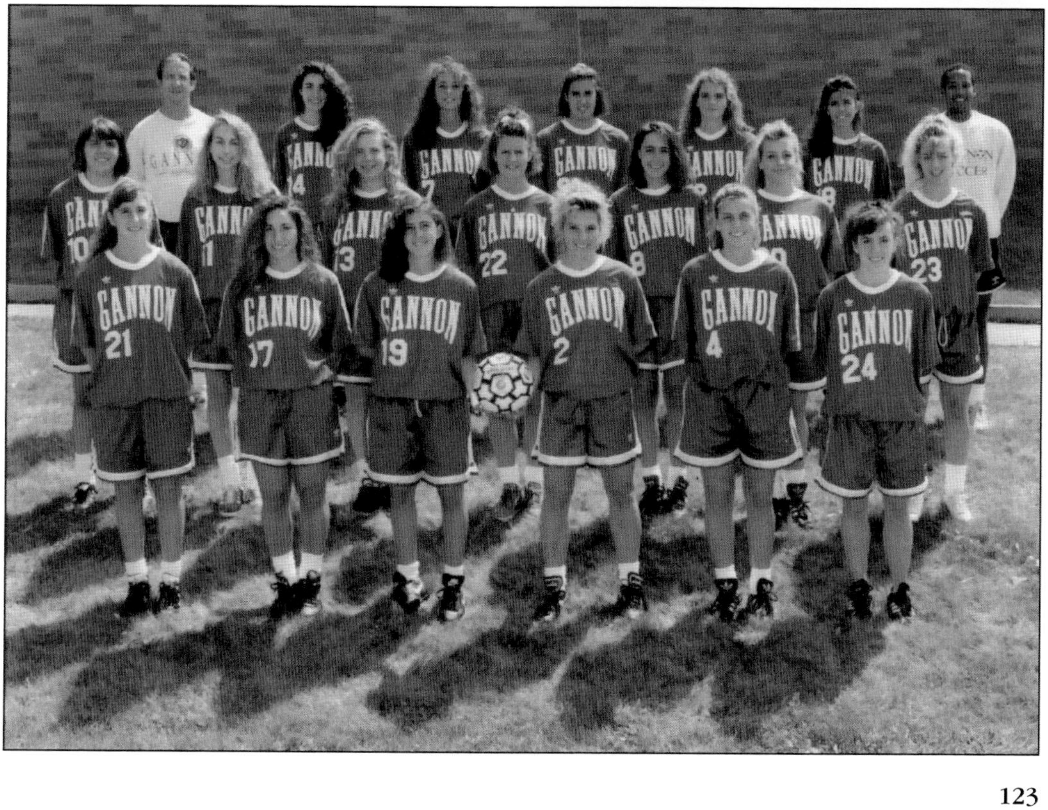

Kathy Wotus Kuhns was an outside hitter for the Gannon volleyball team from 1989 to 1992. She is one of only two Gannon athletes to have their number retired and was inducted into the Athletics Hall of Fame in 2011. While at Gannon, she had 1,293 digs and 1,970 kills and was the school's first American Volleyball Coaches Association All-American, an award she won twice.

The 2010 women's basketball team finished the regular season with a perfect 24-0 record. They went on to play in the NCAA Division II national championship as the number one seed and were ranked number one in the country in the USA Today/ESPN top-25 coach's poll. The team lost the championship game to Emporia State.

Gannon University Field opened in the spring of 2001 when it hosted a women's lacrosse game. The field, which has a seating capacity of 2,500, is also home to Gannon's soccer, softball, baseball, and football teams. In 2015, the field was renamed McConnell Family Stadium when Dennis McConnell, a 1970 alumnus, made a generous donation to the university in honor of his parents.

In 2013, Gannon added competitive cheer to its roster of varsity sports. The sport, which is independent of the game-day cheerleading squads, focuses on partner stunts, pyramids, basket toss, and tumbling. The team has been very successful, appearing in the National Cheer Association Collegiate Cheer Championship every year since its founding.

Acrobatics and Tumbling is an emerging sport that is working to become a fully accredited NCAA championship sport. In 2013, Gannon was only the 10th college in the nation to add this to its roster of varsity sports. In 2018, the university hosted the National Collegiate Acrobatics and Tumbling Association National Championship and won a gold medal in the inversion pyramid event.

Women's wrestling became Gannon's 22nd varsity sport when it was introduced in 2018. The inaugural team had 13 wrestlers and was coached by Christen Dierken, who was a member of the US national team. Gannon is the 39th college in the country to add the sport and the first school in Pennsylvania with a four-year collegiate program.

BIBLIOGRAPHY

Barcio, Rev. Dr. Robert, et al. *The Story of Gannon University Education on the Square*. Erie, PA: Gannon University Press, 1985.

Barcio, Rev. Dr. Robert. *"That You Love One Another" The Life and Times of Archbishop John Mark Gannon.* Erie, PA: Larson Texts, 1995.

Consistent with our mission to preserve history on a local level, this book was printed in South Carolina on American-made paper and manufactured entirely in the United States. Products carrying the accredited Forest Stewardship Council (FSC) label are printed on 100 percent FSC-certified paper.